Mentored by Mind

Soul to Soul Conversations

Also written by

Elsie Spittle

Wisdom for Life

Our True Identity...Three Principles

Beyond Imagination - A New Reality Awaits

Nuggets of Wisdom - Learning to See Them

The Path to Contentment

Nuggets of Wisdom II - Learning & Sharing in Shorthand

Mentored by Mind

Soul to Soul Conversations

Elsie Spittle

Mentored by Mind
Soul to Soul Conversations
by Elsie Spittle

Copyright © 2021 Elsie Spittle
www.3phd.net

ISBN 9798717372510

Published by Amazon Kindle Direct Publishing

All rights reserved. No part of this work covered by the copyrights hereon may be reproduced or used in any form or by any means—graphic, electronic or mechanical—without the prior written permission of the author, except for reviewers who may quote brief passages. Any request for photocopying, recording, taping or storage on information retrieval systems of any part of this work shall be directed in writing to the author.

First printed in 2021
Printed in the USA

Editor: Jane Tucker
Cover design and book layout: Lynn Spittle and Kim Patriquin
Author photo: Lynn Spittle

Note: All client names have been changed to protect their privacy

About the Author

Elsie Spittle was a personal friend of Sydney Banks before he had his epiphany. After initial resistance, she realized the profundity of Syd's discoveries and was the first person to formally share them with the public and mental health professionals.

Elsie went from life as a homemaker to becoming a global consultant and mentor of leading Three Principles practitioners, devoting her life to sharing this transformative mental health paradigm with the world.

She had the privilege of receiving "on the job" training directly from Mr. Banks, travelling with him to address mental health practitioners, educators, and others seeking a deeper understanding of life.

Elsie Spittle is highly regarded as a public speaker because of her ability to reach an audience, large or small, via a "feeling" that touches the heart and soul.

Married for 58 years, with a loving and supportive family, she has her own private business and is co-founder of the Three Principles School, located on Salt Spring Island, BC.

This is Elsie's seventh published book.

Elsie's website: www.3phd.net

Endorsements

What people are saying about *Mentored by Mind:*

"*Mentored by Mind* is a powerfully enriching contribution to enhancing one's level of understanding of the elusive Three Principles of Mind, Consciousness and Thought.

Through a delightful series of moving vignettes, Elsie Spittle lucidly illustrates the difficult to articulate, but potent transformative power of The Three Principles. An abundant variety of stories portray her clients' courage, hope, inspiration, self-trust and their ability to overcome fear and doubt. The stories point to the joy of being your own best friend and mentor; of being guided and empowered by wisdom.

This book is fifty years ahead of its time, representing a paradigm shift from the traditional medical model of mental health. It offers a remedy for the relief of stress by means of enhancing one's mind-body health connection holistically. It disentangles the mind from contaminated personal thinking, differentiating wisdom from ego, leading to innate mental health and self-esteem.

Elsie pours her heart and soul into her writing. She has a warm, motherly way about her that guides her clients' journeys with insight, gentleness, love and understanding.

Savor the richness and wisdom of this book. It will bring you to a deep understanding of life's mysteries.

Be prepared to enjoy reading, reflecting and re-reading this book, tuning in to its simple yet profound and inspiring message."

Dr. Wally Litwa, Board Certified Family Physician, Retired

"*Mentored by Mind* is an honest appreciation of how the Principles work for everyone. The raw vulnerability that Elsie Spittle and her clients share throughout the book remind me we are all the same and that love is the answer for all of us.

Elsie does such a beautiful job of showing us just how vulnerability allows us to connect. The ability to share your soul with another without thinking there is a hierarchy to this approach.

After years studying with Syd, Elsie realized after his passing that she would need to move on without his guidance and she turned inward. This allowed her a whole new experience of herself and her connection to Mind. *Mentored by Mind* is a reminder that it doesn't matter how long you have been involved in the Principles, the gifts go deeper and deeper. Thank you, Elsie."

Cheryl Wilkie, PsyD., MLADC

"Elsie's book *Mentored by Mind* is an invitation to reflect on the limitless potential, love and presence that is always available to guide practitioners and the people we serve. Drawing on personal stories and her direct experience of being mentored by Mind, Elsie shines a light on the most intimate and trusted relationship we could ever have.

If you've ever wanted a deeper, effortless way of aligning your work, service and life with who and what you really are, this book will resonate with you. I read the book slowly and every time I put it down my spirit felt expanded. Elsie's honesty and openness felt like I was with her in person."

Jacquie Moses, Transformational coach, Three Principles practitioner and Speaker

"This book was a joy and privilege to read. In *Mentored by Mind*, whilst joining Elsie for a virtual cup of tea, she takes you gently by the hand through a wondrous selection of soul-to-soul conversations. Lovingly and insightfully pointing you back to your inner essence, Elsie reminds you that YOU are 'Mind' and that it is not separate from you and that this inner guidance system is at work 24/7/365.

In the exquisite sharing of client conversations, you are given exclusive access to your own true nature, your own unique inner essence. Such a gift for humanity."

Maureen York, Three Principles coach, speaker and retreat leader

"*Mentored by Mind* is a book for anyone who wants to experience their true nature more fully and share their love in the world more freely. Elsie Spittle reminds us through her personal stories to start with loving ourselves first.

Mentored by Mind is a soul song to our humanity with each vignette a reminder of the divinity in it all. There are no exceptions. There is no hierarchy. The human and the spiritual are one.

This book helped me to become a better listener to the whispers of my soul. Enjoy the reassuring comfort of Elsie's grandmotherly wisdom. Her common-sense prose contains within it profound spiritual understanding hiding in plain sight. It is a welcome reminder to come home within ourselves and embrace the feeling of our true nature. It is not separate from us. It is who we are."

Rohini Ross, Co-founder of The Rewilders and the Rewilding Love podcast.

Previous Endorsements

"There is a line in *Nuggets of Wisdom II* that epitomises the content of the whole, as well as touching on what Elsie Spittle's writing is so evocative of: 'simplicity versus complexity, of stillness versus noise, of love versus ego.' In this selection of insights, you will be invited to turn your own gaze inwards in order to realise the simplicity, stillness and love that reside there, ever present, and in service of humankind."

Dr Giles P Croft, former NHS surgeon, writer, speaker and Three Principles practitioner.

"If you are in a helping profession of any kind, Elsie's book, *The Path to Contentment*, will speak to you deeply. Throughout, she shares insights and stories that demonstrate the deeper essence of human nature and the profound results that happen when we help people awaken to this Truth. Elsie has been a mentor, friend and inspiration in my own work and I know her words will do the same for you. Elsie exemplifies the richness we experience when we remain students, look in the direction of our True Nature and let Wisdom reveal itself in the everyday ordinariness of our extraordinary lives."

Barbara Patterson, Global Coach & Consultant, Conversations that Transform

"Elsie Spittle is a treasure—warm and wise with a depth of understanding that illuminates human psychology. In her book, *Nuggets of Wisdom*, she shares hundreds of discreet invitations to awaken to our own ultimate resource—the wealth of wisdom within us."

Michael Neill, radio show host and bestselling author of The Inside-Out Revolution.

"Have you ever felt there must be some special meaning to your life, but you didn't know what it was? Through an accident of history, the author of *Our True Identity* was the lifelong friend of a man who suddenly became enlightened. On her inner journey, mentored by Sydney Banks, she found her True Identity. Cherish her words. You just might find yourself hidden within."

Keith Blevens, PhD, Clinical Psychologist, Washington

"*Beyond Imagination* offers readers a unique glimpse into the earliest history of The Three Principles, as awareness of their profound impact grew and began to spread throughout the world.

Elsie Spittle has been a pioneering practitioner in a wide range of areas. This book offers the reader the best of Elsie. You get a sense of her sweetness and caring and her outlook on life.

You can see and feel the influence of Sydney Banks in the flow, feel and focus of the book and it is lovely to see that live on with us through Elsie's work. This book has a lot to offer people new to the Principles understanding, as well as those who want to keep learning more. Thank you, Elsie, for taking the time to share all of this with us."

Aaron Turner PhD, Co-founder and senior partner, One Thought Ltd.

Dedication

This book is dedicated to all the practitioners who share their understanding of the Three Principles around the globe. Whether you share formally as a mental health professional, or in industry or in any other human endeavor, as a parent or spouse, sharing love means something precious. Thank you!

As always, my eternal gratitude to Sydney Banks, Scottish mystic and visionary extraordinaire.

Author's Note

Dear Readers,

I invite you to join me for a virtual cup of tea while I share some true-life transformational stories. In this book, I do my best to speak directly to your heart and soul, true nature speaking with true nature. My hope is that during our visit, something new might occur to you. Relax, put your feet up, and listen to the whisper of your wisdom.

Contents

Introduction	xxiii
Sydney Banks Excerpt	xxv
Part One	1
"See" How Our Inner Wisdom Mentors Us	3
Follow the Feeling and Trust Mind	8
Honor our Bodies and our Souls	12
Listening Without Ego	15
Living in our Understanding	19
Wisdom Energy versus Ego Energy	21
Insights Never Vanish	25
Faith is the Heart of Business	30
Part Two	35
The Power of Seeing	37
Reflection brings Understanding	39
How to Get Unstuck	42
The Light Within	44
Living in Well-Being and Love	46
Our True Nature is our Angel	50
Listening and Sharing in Shorthand	52
The Quiet is the Gold	58

It's a Feeling World	61
Honor What You Do Know	67
Part Three	71
"Seeing" and Standing in Truth	73
Share Clearly and with Love	80
"Seeing" the Beauty Beyond Behavior	83
Feeling the Feeling more than the Words	88
Spiritual Energy is Everything	92
Epilogue	101
Further Reading	103
Resources	104
Acknowledgements	105

Introduction

When Syd came to our home to share the miracle that had occurred to him, the revelation of three spiritual gifts, Mind, Consciousness, and Thought, we felt we were in the presence of the unknown. Something strange and mysterious was embodied in this man who was our friend.

What he shared was completely beyond our understanding, yet we felt entranced by the strength of the feeling emanating from him. This is the gift we all have within—spiritual connection. The gift to touch another's soul, the gift to awaken one's true nature. This is the wonder of the Oneness.

This book was inspired by conversations with clients, groups, family and friends. I am grateful for the insights that were sparked as we learned together. I never fail to be lifted by soul-to-soul connection, and by the resilience and courage of the human spirit.

We humans are a remarkable blend of the ordinary and extraordinary, of the form and the formless. This recognition fills me with wonder and awe. It is my hope that you, the reader, may also be inspired and stirred by the stories contained within. Enjoy!

Sydney Banks Excerpt

"It's nothing new. It's something that's been on this reality since the beginning of time and it's called Truth. And Truth is a spiritual intelligence before the formation of this reality we know.

How do you get to this Truth? How does it become alive? It's really very simple. The Three Principles that bring everything into creation... Divine Mind, Divine Consciousness and Divine Thought. And with Mind, Consciousness and Thought to guide you through life, you learn to use them properly.

Now you don't really have to think about Mind because Mind is the intelligence of all things. You've already got it. Consciousness makes you aware. You're already aware. What's left is Thought and Thought is like the rudder of a ship; it guides you through life. And if you can learn to use that rudder properly, you can guide your way through life way, way better than you ever imagined.

You can go from one reality to another. You can find your happiness. And when illusionary sadness comes from memories, you don't try to figure them out, please don't try and do that, you'll get yourself in trouble. All you have to do is, simplicity again, is realize that it is Thought. The second you realize it's thought it's gone. You're back to the now, you're back to happiness.

So, don't get caught up in a lot of details. In this world, the smaller it is the more powerful it is. And here we have Mind, Consciousness and Thought. That's very simple. That's the answer."

-Sydney Banks 2000

Part One

"See" How Our Inner Wisdom Mentors Us

Over the last decade or so, I've facilitated and spoken on many webinars for organizations. I loved doing this as part of my service. However, it wasn't until a year and half ago that my webmaster, André, shared his thoughts on the importance of my doing webinars on my own as well.

When André first mentioned it to me, I was a doing a retreat in Norway that he attended. André asked to meet with me after the event was over and shared his vision.

I wasn't interested. I was doing a lot of one-on-one mentoring and wasn't keen on doing it online with a group. I admit, I was rather dismissive. I thanked him for offering his ideas and let him know I wasn't moved to take it further.

It was probably a year after that when André asked if he could speak with me. He didn't say what he wanted to talk about; he was rather secretive. When we had our Zoom call, to my surprise, he had a power point presentation of what he envisioned as an online mentoring program for me to offer practitioners.

At first, to be honest, I was a tad annoyed and I told him that I still wasn't really interested. "Yet here you are bringing this up again." What is surprising is that half way through his presentation, I got captivated by what he'd put together. Mind

Elsie Spittle

held me still enough so that I could "hear"' past my intellect and past my beliefs. I was being Mentored by Mind.

I got a feeling for what he was sharing, and the outline he had presented. All of a sudden, without thinking about it, I said, "I'm in." A feeling of freshness and excitement took hold of me and we were away to the races. I began to work with André, adding my own voice to the outline he had developed for me. That's how I started my first online mentoring program, which breathed life into two more online programs.

As I was going through this development process with André, he suggested we have a Facebook chat room, where people could get together between our group calls. This would be a way for people to keep in touch and share insights, ask each other questions, and so forth. André explained that chat rooms were well thought of in current online group calls. Nonetheless, I wasn't a fan of this idea. Again, I felt I was being guided by Mind, via a deep feeling of certainty.

André and I had a conversation about this. I explained that I really appreciate and respect when people share their insights or experiences, and that I'd ask for questions on the calls; however, in between times, I really wanted people to have that time to talk with themselves—to talk and listen to their own wisdom.

Mentored by Mind

As André and I explored the importance of people tuning into their own wisdom, he really got it as an insight. As it turned out, the people who signed up for the program loved the idea of *not* having a chat room, of having time off to simply "be and learn" more from themselves. A lesson to be valued for life.

Believe me, I know how easy it is to go to someone else for an answer. When I was learning from Syd, I counted on him for answers to my questions. There were certainly moments throughout my learning when I had insights while I was working with a group, or just on my own; where I felt I was being mentored by Mind in the moment. However, later in the day, my intellect would come into play and I'd start to second guess myself. I would call Syd to share what had happened during the program. I'd ask, "Was I right?" I counted on him to tell me whether I was right or not. . . sometimes he answered my questions; other times he said, *"Trust your own wisdom."*

Syd passed over a decade ago, in May, 2009. I feel in some ways that since his passing, I've learned as much, if not more, than I did in the thirty years previously when I had the privilege of being mentored by him.

Now, I no longer had Syd as my "go to" man; my mentor. This was a real shift in my consciousness, in my understanding, and I found myself listening more deeply to Mind—listening to my own wisdom.

Elsie Spittle

As my listening deepened, I found more patience. I used to be a compulsive-impulsive type of person. When some idea or thought would come to me, I didn't take time to reflect. I'd jump on it and often times in my impulsiveness, I innocently hurt people. There were times I lashed out in anger or made decisions as head of an organization without discussing the issues with the rest of the team. I had no idea that consulting with the team and employees brought about a sense of ownership and responsibility from the group.

When I started to learn more from my own wisdom, it brought me a sense of calmness and clarity, and a feeling that there was no rush. I had this mantra come to me: "If you don't know—wait until you know." I've never come to a time when I've had to make an immediate decision; where there wasn't some time to pause and reflect for a moment or more. Perhaps you have and I respect that.

Certainly, I'd get out of the way if a car was careening toward me or if my brakes failed or whatever. I don't mean to be flippant. I'm trying to convey that as patience began to be released within me, I learned to trust that when I don't know how to handle something or what the next step is, the time will come when I'll know. And I'm content to wait.

This deeper Mind knowledge has lessened my compulsion to "do." It has moved me more into "being;" into trusting that it is okay to be in the unknown. As a result, being

Mentored by Mind

in the unknown has become more comfortable. This new knowledge has created a truly beneficial shift. It has given me the confidence to trust myself.

Follow the Feeling and Trust Mind

Prior to the start of my second online program, "Mentored by Mind," there were two responses to my brief questions that really stood out for me. It was interesting to note that some participants didn't even know why they were joining. A typical response was, "I don't know why; I just feel drawn to it."

The other response was that they all wanted to go deeper, combined with their respect for a "feeling." They trusted the feeling that prompted them to join without knowing why! I found that fascinating and wonderful; proof that "feeling" is the observable expression and guidance of Mind.

It's a simple thing, this "feeling" of being in the moment, knowing you can count on Mind to guide; and it's very practical. For example, as practitioners, we can feel comfortable not having to prepare so much for a presentation or a webinar, knowing that Mind will guide.

Sometimes, I'll have insights in the middle of the night prior to sharing online or whatever the case may be. Other times, I'll feel I'm a blank slate, with nothing on my mind. Regardless of insights or not, I always take at least ten or fifteen minutes prior to starting, where I allow myself time to be still, to be quiet. That quiet space is primarily where Mind speaks via insight. Or via a feeling. That deep feeling is like an

Mentored by Mind

insight without words. Allowing space for Mind to emerge shows our respect and love for Mind; for our wisdom.

Having said that, I want you to know that quiet or stillness isn't a requirement in order to be guided by wisdom. Sometimes, in the midst of chaos, panic, or anger, Mind will come through. I know this, as it did for me after resisting Syd's teachings for over a year. Many of you know that I became so upset with him that I never wanted to see the man again! In that feeling of upset and lostness, when I saw him and his late wife, Barb, driving up to our home, I wanted to lock the door so he couldn't enter. I didn't do that. Instead, I hid in the bathroom as I felt safe there. Yet in my fear, without my volition, I was moved to leave my safe place and greet the Banks' at the front door. That episode was the turning point for me. Shortly after Syd left, leaving me with beautiful words of hope, I remained in the midst of fear and anger. Then, without seeking, insight blossomed for me, and my life changed in an instant.

As did the life of one of the participants, who, prior to signing up for the program, asked me whether she should join us or not. We exchanged several emails, and finally, I said to her, "Listen to yourself. Trust your own wisdom. It's you who must make that decision."

Ultimately, she said, "Elsie, when you told me to make my own decision, I felt like you'd left me all alone, like I was hiding in the bathroom, as you were when you hid from Syd. And I had to run out and say, "I'll join." And that's what she did. And gaining insight on the calls enriched her life. It's another example of how Mind shows up in the most unusual ways, when least expected.

As I said before, although I allow myself more time to be still and receive Mind guidance, I also know for certain that you can be absolutely caught up in your thinking and feel there's no hope, and Mind will still come through.

"Why do you think that is?" is the question I posed to my Mentored by Mind group.

One of the participants, I'll call her Tracy, said this: "Mind is what I'm made of. Mind never goes away. It's not something that comes and goes. If I'm caught up in my thinking, that's okay; it doesn't mean anything about Mind not being there because it can't not be there; I'm made of it. So, I can always trust Mind."

I loved Tracy's response. Yes, we can always trust Mind. Mind touching minds or soul-to-soul connection. The more that spiritual fact came through to me, that we live in Mind—that's who we are—the healthier I got, both spiritually and physically. Even though I'm going in and out of that wellness physically, Mind continues to guide me in that regard too. I began to listen to the whisper of wisdom telling me I was

Mentored by Mind

travelling too much. I was so enamored with serving that I forgot to take care of myself. Does that sound familiar to anybody?

Ah yes, you know we're so alike in so many ways. Not just because we're made of the same spiritual energy, but because we all, at one time or another, fall into the same seductive trap about being able to serve humanity, to serve the world, sometimes at the exclusion of serving ourSelf.

The mission in churches and for social service providers is to help, to assist humanity. That was one of Syd's strongest teaching points, after his epiphany. He said countless times, *"This understanding will assist humanity and alleviate anxiety and stress."* He also made the bold statement that *"These Principles have the power to change the fields of psychology and psychiatry."*

Honor our Bodies and our Souls

Syd knew that the ultimate benefit of these three Principles was to help humanity understand how to alleviate their stress, and how to live with love and understanding. He also said to take care of our bodies as well as our souls. He shared this with me several times.

At one point when I was visiting him in the hospital, he said, with a smile on his face, *"Don't do what I've done in regard to giving so much of my time and energy that my physical health has started to fail. Take care of yourself. Be good to your body and soul."*

I did see that over the years, he gave his time without question, without complaining. He just gave and gave and gave of his body. And his soul. That was his path. And I did see that his body was failing. Even so, he never gave up hope. He never despaired. He continued to serve humanity right until the end of his time on earth. He saw people while he was in the hospital. He saw people when he was bedridden. He did this with joy, humility, and love.

Although he said, *"Don't do what I did,"* that advice went right over my head. I thought to myself, "Okay, good to know, Syd. Thank you." Then I proceeded to ignore his counsel.

However, in the past year, starting prior to my last London conference in June 2019, my body has begun to really shake

Mentored by Mind

me up and make me notice that I need to take care of myself. I began to get a glimmer that my body, and all of our bodies, are temples for our souls. Our bodies are temples for this spiritual knowledge that lies within.

I used to be dismissive of my body. My thoughts ran like this: "Well, if I'm this spiritual being, I can override my aches and pains and my tiredness because I'm super mom; I'm super woman; I'm super wife. I can do it all."

And I did do it all, for a number of years, actually for 43 years. Until finally my body and wisdom gave me a kick in the behind. For the first time, I paid a little bit of attention; I minimized my travels somewhat, but not enough, and so my body continued to speak to me in stronger terms, both physically and mentally. I experienced more pain in my body. My mind was telling me in no uncertain terms, to "Wake up, lady."

That summer, after the conference in 2019, I took my first 2-month sabbatical, to rest my body and my mind. To rejuvenate and replenish the well. Time to allow Mind to fill the well to the brim, for new learning and insights.

I feel privileged that I've been able to take the summer off for the last couple of years. My time off is never what I think it's going to be, where I'm going to have complete space and have nothing to do. There are still some mentoring calls

Elsie Spittle

that I take when I'm guided by the feeling to do so. Some personal, and some more global.

I had a couple of practitioners from another country who were translating, with permission, Syd's book, *The Missing Link*. They wanted to have a conversation with me as they were finishing it, to talk over a couple of passages. I couldn't turn it down; that inner feeling drew me, the feeling of seeing this book translated and available to citizens of another country. The feeling warmed my heart and soul.

It was a wonderful conversation. And in that hour I spent with them, truly, my body did feel elevated, healthy, and my spirit was uplifted. I was in a different world. Then, later on, my body again was needing some attention. And I honored what my body needed. I rested.

Listening Without Ego

What came to me in the last week of my summer sabbatical was that I'd been creating stress for myself about a project I'd committed to in the coming year. I had agreed to go back to London to do a wonderful program for a group. However, Mind was telling me, "Elsie, you need to rest."

My ego and intellect were saying "Go ahead; do it." My rationale was, if I flew business class, I could stretch out in the reclining sleeper seat and that would be better for my body. Makes sense, right? I kept trying to convince myself I could do it. Ego told me, "You're strong. And the group needs you." Oh my, how seductive the ego can be.

Wisdom is stronger. I woke up the next morning, after being torn by indecision throughout the night, and I knew, "I've got to cancel this trip." I actually posted something on Facebook about the insight I had that when we feel driven beyond our limits, is it wisdom energy or is it ego energy? In that insight, I saw that I was committed more to my ego and the feeling that I can't let this group down, than I was committed to honoring the vessel of Mind. I woke up to a deeper feeling of respect, and "knowing" that I'm not indispensable. My body needed rest.

I realized that I can talk via Zoom, with beautiful souls around the world, in the comfort of my home, and still rest my body; more so than being on a plane for 9 hours and then

Elsie Spittle

pouring out the energy being with people for 4 days. Much as I love doing this, I came to the insightful conclusion that my body was crying out for rest, and I needed to listen to that.

My insight was so strong that I didn't even wait a day or two, which I typically do, to be certain this was the right decision. I just went ahead and let the group in London know what was in my heart and my soul. I felt immediate relief after that call. And the group completely understood and supported my decision.

I'm sure you all have experienced making a difficult decision when the feeling is right, and wisdom is holding your hand, guiding you during uncertainty. I applaud you!

Another beautiful result from the insight of listening to body wisdom was that the stress I'd been experiencing, which wasn't helping my body, began to slowly ease. It felt like a weight off my body, because I was honoring my body as well as my soul. I never knew so deeply, until this past couple of months, that our body is as important as our soul. I really want you, the readers, to hear that. Our body and soul are One; the body is the expression of our spiritual essence.

The other thing that really struck me happened when I spent some time with my daughter, Lynn, and her wife, Kim, a couple of weeks after cancelling my trip to London. They knew I'd been struggling with some physical mobility issues, but they

Mentored by Mind

didn't realize how much, not having seen me in person for quite awhile.

I took them to a live production of Mamma Mia, and after sitting for an hour, I used my cane to get up. They were taken aback by this, although they didn't say anything at the time.

After the show, I let them know I had cancelled my trip to London, and my daughter said "Oh Mama, I'm so glad that you're honoring your needs." Kim nodded her head vigorously. And I thought, wow, out of the mouths of our children!

Lynn said she was shocked to see what was happening with me, and that they both could see I wasn't listening to my body. Both Lynn and Kim were so kind and tender when they gently told me off for not paying more attention to my physical needs.

Ken had been after me for some time to care for my body and not to travel so much, to give myself time to rest. I must admit I said, "Yes, dear," then continued to ignore him. . .The experience of being mentored by Mind, via my family, was truly a wake-up call. To this day, I listen much more deeply to my body/soul wisdom, and to my family.

I hope this is resonating with you, the readers. It's so important. Taking care of yourself, in terms of honoring your body as well as your soul, is about being in service to your

Elsie Spittle

Self. By capitalizing "S", clearly, I don't mean just caring for the little self, although that's part of it.

Sometimes when I talk about Self care, people take that to mean personal self care. I respect that; however, what many clients say to me when I mention "Self care" is this: "When I get stressed, I have a bath, and I have my tablet, and my phone in there with me." That's not really a rest if you have your tablet and your phone in the bathroom with you.

When I mean Self, I'm talking about the spiritual Self. Now, consider that our body also is that spiritual energy manifest into form. That's why we want to celebrate our physical nature as much as we do our spiritual nature. In reality, when we honor our spiritual Self, we honor our physical self. This is honoring the Oneness.

Living in our Understanding

Listening to Mind, and taking care of our Self, as well as our personal self, makes a huge difference in our life. It's as important as the difference between talking about the Principles, versus "living in our understanding."

There are people who may be more articulate than we are. Living in understanding isn't about our ability to "articulate" the Principles. It's the "living" that speaks louder than words. It's the "deep feeling" coming from inside; the feeling of living in our wisdom. Other people will notice and feel that; it gives them hope that their lives can transform as well.

That's what happened for me with Syd. I hated what he was talking about to me. I hated it because the strength and Truth of his wisdom demolished my whole belief system. Yet, I could not turn away from him, because there was something about his living that was so different from the way he lived before.

Most of you will know that I knew Syd before he had his Enlightenment. The way he was living after his transformation, the way he loved his family, the way he loved life, the way he appeared in life physically, the way he took care of himself, was vastly different from before.

Elsie Spittle

The way his humanness changed really struck me, because his humanness still came out and got attached to various situations from time to time; however, his ability to bounce back to wisdom from reactivity spoke to me more than his words. I saw and felt his resilience. Seeing this really moved me, because my characteristic was to hang onto my anger, to hang onto my upset. That's the way I was brought up. I didn't know any better.

What continues to amaze me is that I could be touched, not only by Syd's spiritual nature manifesting in the improvement of the quality of his living, but in the improvement of the quality of his humanness, the resilience of his ability to bounce back from his human frailties.

Equally amazing to me was that my true nature, my own wisdom, was waking up, even during the time when I was arguing with Syd, asking him not to talk to me about this nonsense. Syd's true nature was bypassing my resistance, and speaking directly to my true nature, via the deep feeling emanating from within him.

Wisdom Energy versus Ego Energy

Acknowledging our human frailties can be a real gift, for the relief it brings when we bypass ego and admit, "Yes, I'm not super mom or super woman or super man." The relief we experience when we acknowledge that we have physical needs we want to take care of; and the relief when we honor those needs.

I've learned a lot about humility in the last while, in regard to the physical form; things that I've not learned before. I've been a student of this understanding for close to 45 years and there's still so much more—it never ends.

There's so much more to learn, just in terms of the simple act of living; perhaps living with a little more grace and appreciation, with a little less ego each step of the way.

I'll share a story with you. This happened before my family took me to task for not taking better care of my Self, as I wrote in an earlier chapter. I have a walking cane that was given to me a few years ago. It's the prettiest, collapsible cane, decorated with images of butterflies and flowers. My friend gave it to me, as she observed that I had some difficulty walking. I was about to travel to London, as I often did, to speak at a conference. I wasn't sure if I could walk up the stairs to the stage, and my friend said, "Well, ask someone to help you."

Elsie Spittle

I recoiled as she said that, and hastened to say, "Oh, I couldn't do that. I'd be embarrassed." And she said to me, "Elsie, you know what they say, 'Pride goeth before a fall.'"

Well, I don't know if you've ever heard that old saying, but I'm here to tell you, she was right on target. She caught me in my ego, and chastised me with love. I heard her. And so I did ask a kind man to help me up on the stage. My ego had slipped away and it felt good to make it easier on myself.

The next time I went to London in June, 2019, I took my cane with me, and I was so grateful to have the help. People were so kind when they saw me walking down the long hallway in the airport, and asked if they could assist me. Going into the lounge, again, someone came to support me. People were so thoughtful and helpful; I thought to myself, "This is pretty cool."

I was so touched at the kindness I experienced; it was totally unexpected. I discovered there are gifts when we move past ego and find a little bit more humility; unexpected gifts. Not only in terms of people being kind to me, but the gift of the release of stress, from ego, and from pride. I never knew you could benefit so greatly from humility.

There's a difference between a sense of pride and "rising to the occasion" coming from our innate mental health, versus the pride that comes from ego; for example, thinking, when

Mentored by Mind

our body is crying out for rest, "I'm strong, I can do this. I can surpass my tiredness."

There's a real difference—the difference is in the feeling. When we take a moment or two to be still, we can tell the difference between the energy from ego, or the energy from wisdom. Energy from wisdom feels softer, yet is still a very powerful feeling.

Another example comes to mind of wisdom energy versus ego energy. I was sharing what I was learning about this topic with another client, Myles, during our monthly call. He was very quiet after I'd shared what was new to me.

"How is this sitting with you, Myles? You seem very thoughtful."

Myles: "Yes, I'm in quite a reflective space right now. I think the question that you raised about the discernment of ego energy and wisdom energy is really stirring me. I'm overly familiar with ego energy but I'm becoming more aware of that quality of energy in me and others, and more aware of my response to that feeling. I'm finding it quite uncomfortable a lot of the time, so I'm physically noticing that I'm way out of sync when that happens.

"How can I return to peace and stillness to allow wisdom to guide me?" Myles asked. "I'd love to have more faith and be more grounded in my work. I've just come from giving 3

Elsie Spittle

days of coaching and leadership sessions, and I was in ego a lot. I'm thinking about it now, and wondering how could I have been more in my quiet space, and more trusting of wisdom?"

Elsie: "You know what I love about what you've just shared, Myles? First of all, your honesty and your vulnerability, that you would share what you just did. Thank you.

"Secondly, the fact that you're noticing your response to ego energy is very significant. I suspect you judge yourself for noticing, rather than celebrating that you're noticing. Do you know what I mean?"

Myles shook his head, so I continued. "Instead of judging yourself, with thoughts like 'I could have done better' or 'I was in my ego', honor the fact that you noticed; noticing is the gift of Consciousness. When you 'see' without judging yourself, and without blame, you've got freedom.

"I guarantee the next time you do another program or another session, you won't be the same person. I guarantee that, Myles. It's just that switch from judging yourself for noticing ego to honoring the fact that Consciousness has shown you this. And you say, 'Thank you.' You feel that, don't you? I can tell by the look on your face that you feel the truth of that."

Myles: "Hell, yes!"

Insights Never Vanish

Here is another important spiritual fact that I'd like to share with you. Insights never vanish, and they never get old. Too often we have an insight and think, "Oh wow, this insight has been transformative and has changed my life. My relationships are better; I don't dislike this person any more; I understand that they were functioning from insecurity just like I was," and so on.

After awhile we may feel like the insight has finished its job. We've changed to a degree; now we're in a hurry for the next insight. Patience! Here's where we want to learn and "see" that insights never vanish and never become old.

We *are* insight. The insight has come from within us. It's always nestled in that pure spiritual essence that we're made of and rises to the surface, often when we least expect it. I've had many examples of that, as I'm sure you have too. Perhaps you had a bit of a blind spot, just like me, where we didn't fully comprehend something in our life.

For example, the Oneness, and how the Three Principles are One. That's a beautiful thought. However, that thought was completely over my head when Syd would talk about this. I remember people would ask Syd, and I felt the same, "Why do you say there are Three Principles, if they're all the same?" Syd's reply: *"Because that's how it was revealed to me—that the Three are One."*

Elsie Spittle

Well, I never understood what he meant. When he made that statement, I could feel the truth of that fact resonating within me, but I had absolutely no understanding what it meant. Until 38 years later.

Some of you may have heard this story before. If so, I hope you don't mind my sharing it again. I love the fact that 38 years after my first insight, "Thought creates feeling," I learned something new from that same insight. The first time, I thought I was getting a glimmer of one principle—Thought. That insight was profound to me. It was life changing to realize that Thought creates feeling. To realize that it was my thought, that I'm thought in action—that I'm creating that feeling—that realization put me in the driver's seat.

I began to see that my situation wasn't a result of the family, my upbringing, or my circumstances. I began to understand that it's my ability to think that allows me to create my experience. That was amazing to me. That one insight started my journey, after a year and a half of very strong resistance.

Almost four decades later, I was talking to a group in England; there were many new people, and they said, "Elsie, how did you come into this understanding; what's your story?"

While I was sharing my first insight about Thought, in that moment, all those years later, I realized more fully that Mind

Mentored by Mind

was part of that insight because that's where wisdom comes from—Mind. Mind is where insight is born. Thought brought that insight to life for me, and Consciousness was also at work because it made me aware of the insight. All Three Principles were working together to bring me one simple insight.

I had no idea when the first insight occurred to me that Three were working as One. Initially, I thought my insight was based solely on Thought. While talking with the group I realized, to a degree, the Oneness of the 3 Principles. That there was no separation. Three are One.

When I realized that in front of the audience, I was so elated that I burst out laughing. I felt so much joy in getting a little taste of the Oneness, of the simplicity. Thirty-eight years after my first insight, I realized that we never lose any insight, and that insights can and do continue to blossom throughout our lives. Whenever any one of us or anyone in the world has an insight, the Three Principles are working together to bring that spiritual blessing to us.

I'll give you another example of how insights don't go away or get old. They are permanently nestled within our souls. A few years after the moment when I realized more about the Oneness with the group in England, I experienced a new understanding from that same first insight: Thought creates feeling.

Elsie Spittle

I was giving a talk at a conference in Los Angeles. My topic was, *Mentored by Mind*. I was sharing with the audience how moved I had been when I had that insight. After so much resistance to what Syd had been sharing, during an episode of great anger and fear, to have this beautiful gift blossom in my mind was completely beyond my experience or comprehension. All I knew in the moment was what I felt. I was filled with such relief and joy that I wept. For the first time in my life, I felt worthy. That's the only way I can describe it.

As I was sharing this with the audience, it struck me like a light bulb going on in my head. What's a feeling of worthiness if not innate mental health? And I realized that was also part of the "Thought creates feeling" insight.

What was so wonderous to me in that moment in Los Angeles, is that I had experienced the feeling of innate health, without realizing it at the time. I didn't know that the feeling of worthiness was innate mental health! I was innocently ignorant of how we humans' function, and what we all are made of. I had no idea at the time that we are born with innate mental health. And I didn't realize until my talk in Los Angeles, that I was experiencing wellbeing in that early insight, manifesting in relief and joy. I just felt those feelings without connecting them to well-being.

Do you see what I'm saying about how one insight can continue to flesh out, to get deeper and deeper, no matter

Mentored by Mind

how many years have gone by? There I was in LA, 44 years later, when I realized the feeling of worthiness was innate mental health.

I share this story because I trust that as you read this, your true nature is going to be stirring and giving you more understanding. When this happens, you'll be seeing life with more depth. There will be insights coming to you where you will realize that an insight you had a while back is even more profound than you had thought.

Faith is the Heart of Business

I love being a student and learning with a client. I remember having an amazing conversation with a young man called Nathan. I'd been mentoring him for a few sessions.

What I'd observed during the course of our conversation was that Nathan had been struggling with developing the new arm of his business. He'd been trying to control the situation with his intellect.

Then he realized, in his words, "I needed to take my hands off the wheel and have faith. I realized that I didn't necessarily have to teach my clients about the Principles right off the bat. It occurred to me that it's where I come from; it's my presence with my team and clients, that's more important. It's my living the Principles that teaches, without having to share words so much."

Nathan paused for a moment, then continued. "I know there may be a point where I do share my understanding more formally with them, but I saw that more than anything, the example is my living in wellbeing. That's the big difference."

"That's beautiful, Nathan. I really appreciate what you've learned."

A lovely silence filled the space for a few moments, then I asked Nathan if it was okay to carry on. With his permission,

Mentored by Mind

I inquired about an insight he'd shared toward the end of our previous call. "Do you remember, Nathan? You talked about how you're seeing faith in business, and I wondered how that is unfolding."

"Oh yes, wow, that was quite some insight!" Nathan exclaimed. "I remember it became so clear in the middle of my talk with you, Elsie; I got so excited. I could see that faith in my private life is a good thing. I had faith that this situation will sort itself out, and everything will be fine.

"But in running my business I've always been a grinder, especially when things are hard. When things are tough, ahhh there's not much faith in my heart, I can promise you that.

"But it hit me like a ton of bricks when I spoke with you, Elsie, that faith is what deepens our ability to do something really cool in our business. It deepens our understanding about our business. I started to see that if I don't have faith in business, things take more time. If I'm not having faith, I'm starting to fiddle with it. I'm thinking that this specific process is going too slow; then I'm thinking that now we need to do this, or maybe that, and I start to grind on things." Nathan gave a big sigh. "It's exhausting!"

"Now I'm starting to see that faith is what's given my business the opportunity to grow and expand organically," Nathan said. "Taking my hand off the steering wheel was so

Elsie Spittle

radical to me, Elsie. As you could tell from my response when we talked that last session, I was like, Elsie, I need to tell you something! Is this possible? Can faith really be so productive?

"I remember you were smiling and happy for me. You said, 'That's excellent, Nathan. I love that.'"

I know it's important to draw the wisdom out of my clients, to hear them express what they're learning, so that it really becomes visible. I invited Nathan to say more. "In our conversation, you also mentioned heart; that faith brings the heart back into business. That really resonated with me. Could you say a bit more about that?"

Nathan: "Thank you so much for reminding me of that because that is so true. I was wondering, do I dare to be myself, to bring my true self into business, into conversations, and share my faith? Then it dawned on me, that simply being myself is more powerful and impactful than trying to get my clients to understand what I'm talking about, when I'm trying to share the Principles. I realized that just being myself was enough; to have faith that my true nature would engage their true nature.

"I began to understand that if I come from a feeling of wellbeing, from my heart, that this has great impact in business. We don't have to force sales or any of the tactics that we used to do. We can just show up and be our self.

Mentored by Mind

"This is a completely different mind set than the old school I came from. You know, hustle and grind, tactics and strategies, and wishing for success. I call it old school. I don't mean to insult anybody. But to me, it's just the old grind of my upbringing and my education on how to do business; compared to being true to our inner self in business."

Elsie: "I agree, Nathan. It's like the best of both worlds. I can see that there are times where we have insights about a strategy or a goal. When that strategy is coming from insight, there's no stress attached to it. When I used to do projects for organizations or for communities, I had to put together a proposal, an outline with goals and objectives, and I did it. I played the game, within the system. I provided the information necessary for funders and other game players to see what we were doing. And when I was actually with people, I was in the moment. I was in the feeling of wellbeing, as much as possible.

"Even during times when somebody might challenge me from the audience, I could still find a way to pause for a moment, and re-group. That break would allow me to get grounded, then I could come back in and address whatever it was the person had a question about.

"I want to add that in terms of meeting goals and objectives, there were times where we didn't meet the goals we had put on paper. We had to answer to the foundations and the investors who had donated funds to a community project.

"When we met with them, we acknowledged that was true; we hadn't met all the goals we'd identified. Our honesty cleared our minds so we could see there was one goal that we hadn't anticipated that showed up in the post evaluation.

To our surprise and delight, the percentage of teen pregnancy in the community had decreased substantially. As the girls in the community, who were learning about the Principles, uncovered their innate mental health, their natural self esteem, they were learning to say "no" to finding love in all the wrong places because they had more respect for themselves.

"The foundations and investors loved that. They respected our honesty, that we didn't try to cover up that we hadn't met all the proposal goals, yet a very essential community culture had begun to change.

"Our honesty and the unanticipated results saved us, and they continued to fund the program. When we play the game with love, respect, and honesty, we won't go far off track."

Part Two

The Power of Seeing

One of the things I've noticed in my mentoring calls is how often people miss what they "see." They are aware of their behaviors and the beliefs that they currently have; even beliefs about the 3 Principles. However, they often are innocent about their "seeing." So, in this segment, I'd like to focus on the power of "seeing."

In Part One, the segment entitled *Wisdom Energy versus Ego Energy,* I shared an example of a client, Myles, who was concerned about the ego he saw in himself. He voiced his concerns with courage and with humility. Myles was bothered by how he'd noticed his ego in the leadership sessions he had offered his clients.

He told me this in a way that came across as if he were judging himself because of what he'd noticed. I find it endearing when my clients tell me what they "see" without knowing what they are "seeing;" I'm touched by their innocence.

I coached Myles on the value of "noticing" and pointed out that noticing is "seeing" from the principle of Consciousness. It's a gift to be able to "see" our behavior, without attachment, without judgment.

Sometimes when we view our behavior, and perhaps it's not the best behavior, the human tendency is to judge it.

Elsie Spittle

Myles' words indicated that he felt an ego energy. The fact that he noticed that was so powerful. That was a gift.

Now, in order to go a step deeper into the gift of Consciousness, it's important to acknowledge where "seeing" comes from. It isn't so much about what we see, it's where that "seeing" comes from. When we realize where "seeing" comes from, we're living in our wisdom, we're living in the Principles, we're living in Mind.

When we honor where "seeing" comes from, we're honoring the source. This releases Mind to function with more freedom within us, as a human and spiritual being. Thus, Mind guides us more readily in our life, offering more depth of understanding. I trust this makes sense to you.

Reflection brings Understanding

When I see and feel people getting reflective, even if their understanding may not be visible to them, the reflection they're experiencing tells me they're getting it—whether they understand or not. That's the moment to trust that now they will teach themselves. Their reflective state of mind IS the teaching; it's utilizing the Universal education contained within.

I'll never forget, and it still brings a smile to my face, when Syd would pause as he'd look around the meeting room at us students in the early days, seeing our wrinkled brows as we'd be sitting there trying so hard to understand his words with our intellect.

Then he'd grin that endearing grin of his, and say, *"You know you don't have to understand this in order to get it, right? Just relax and enjoy the feeling. If you're getting the feeling, you're getting the understanding."*

And I'm thinking, "Well, how can that be? We've all been taught as children by our parents, then at school, at university, that we need to understand, that we need to learn with our intellect. That's the traditional way of education. So to be told we don't have to understand and we'll still get it seemed impossible to me."

Then I began to "see" how a deep positive feeling actually brings to life a new perspective. This insight paved the way to

Elsie Spittle

trusting the feeling more, and not paying as much attention to the "How can this be?" I had the proof in front of me. My perspective and the quality of life I was leading was changing.

I remember, during a session with Jenny, asking her why we could learn via a feeling rather than trying to figure things out. She didn't have an answer. In previous sessions, she had struggled with trying to analyze her thinking in order to resolve problems she was experiencing in life, and in the process, getting more gripped by her thinking. I let her know that trusting the feeling more would enhance her learning and her life.

When I posed that earlier question to her this time, she said, "Because we ARE it. We don't have to understand it because we ARE the answer." She paused momentarily, looking a bit puzzled at her reply. "It's odd, Elsie. I know that's the answer. I feel it. I just don't understand it." Then her face brightened, and she smiled as she said, "And I don't care!"

We both chuckled at the paradox. To know the answer, yet not understand.

Jenny said, "Elsie, could you say a little more about this?"

I was still for a time, then responded, "There's a little gap between our intellect and our wisdom. This is natural. It's like the gap between inside and outside. And sometimes that gap will come together with an inner bang! And you'll have an

Mentored by Mind

insight, an "aha" moment. At that moment, you'll be past reflection and you'll be into knowing.

"Then another level of understanding opens for you; you may not be able to articulate it. You may think, "Okay, I got it!" Then it floats away like a feather in the wind. What did you get? You're not sure?

"You may tell yourself, "I know, I know that this is so, I have a knowing about it, a sense about it, but I don't know how to say it. I don't know how to articulate it."

Jenny is nodding enthusiastically at my words, and she bursts out, "I've had that happen to me many times. I just didn't know what to do with it. Knowing, but not knowing how to express my knowing!"

"That's beautiful, Jenny. That knowing is wisdom, and wisdom brings our understanding to life. There are so many facets to this understanding. Just when you think, "Okay, now I get how it works," it flips on you. Mind flips on you and gives you another avenue, another way to hear and see. And at first, you may think, "Oh come on Mind, give me a break. Am I never going to understand?"

How to Get Unstuck

"As soon as we hit a plateau and think "I've got it," this is usually the time where it's easy to get stuck in what we think we know. I see you're nodding, Jenny. How do you know when you're stuck?"

Jenny: "For me, it feels like it's too hard. Whatever I'm doing is just way too hard. And I keep trying to get out of it, but it just gets harder."

Elsie: "What are you learning about that now?"

Jenny: "When I was first learning about the Principles, I would tell myself, 'I should know better; but how do I let go? Then somehow, I got it. I did it. I didn't learn, I did it. And then something else would happen, and I forgot how to let go. Once again, the judgment came—I should know better. I've done it in the past, I should know how to let go. So, it just comes and goes.

"I'm not so attached to the judgment. What I found and trust is that wisdom, as I picture it, is as if it's a little angel or just a light. It's right here, and the answer is here. The beauty of being human is the freedom to just bang my head on a wall, if I want to. And wisdom will be here when I decide to let it in and I stop banging my head. And oh my, what a relief!"

Mentored by Mind

Jenny exhaled, and once again, we both chuckled. My heart filled in response to her honesty, and her humanness. It's not everyone who would see banging one's head against a wall as the freedom to be human. And to say that without blaming herself, but just as a matter-of-fact observation.

"I really appreciate your response, Jenny. There are two things I hear from you. The first thing I heard you say was, 'I don't know how I let go, but somehow, I did it.' To me the key word is 'somehow.' Me too! There are times when I don't know how to let go, yet somehow, I know. When I get stuck and I've had enough, there's a shift. It's that simple. It's not that I do anything; it's what Syd used to call *'doing without doing.'* Somehow, there's a shift in our understanding. It's part of our innate well-being that rises to the surface again. And we can count on this spiritual process; it's completely reliable.

"To me, not knowing also speaks to keeping us humble. It keeps us humble because we don't always know. And that's okay. There's an aliveness to not knowing. And yet not knowing doesn't hold us back from evolving spiritually and mentally. I love that!"

The Light Within

"The second thing that struck me, Jenny, is I want you to take that light you spoke of, that's beside you, and place it right over you and in you. Own your wisdom. Own that you are the angel. That is so important.

"When you talk about the angel or the light, I want you to recognize that the angel and the light are inside of you, inside of us all. It's another way of saying that we're the Principles in action, we're wisdom in action. We're It.

"At one time, I used to feel that wisdom had my back. Or wisdom was shoulder to shoulder with me when life challenges came up. I didn't see that wisdom didn't just have my back; wisdom is my back!

"Let me explain it this way, Jenny. My husband had stage four cancer a number of years ago. I found a degree of solace as I felt wisdom had my back and Ken's back. And then I began to see that while Ken was going through this, he was living "inside" more than I was. He's a very modest, quiet man, and rather reserved until he gets to know you. The example of his quietly living in wisdom, staying calm and positive, showed me there was something deeper for me to see, deeper than talking about it. Ken didn't talk about it; he just was It. He was wisdom in action, without words. As I observed Ken living more in his wisdom, this helped calm me down.

Mentored by Mind

"That's the beauty of owning our wisdom. I don't mean 'own' as an ego-based owning, like I'm so great to own my wisdom. I mean 'own' as a sacred gift. To 'own' feels like part of 'to honor.' When we honor our wisdom fully, we acknowledge that we're wisdom, and we acknowledge it by feeling how blessed we are to have this sacred gift. The gift of being part of this spiritual essence. And because we're part of it, there is no separation. That's where that Oneness comes in; we're part of the Oneness."

A deep feeling of peace came over me, and I could see that Jenny was affected as well. Her face was serene, her body relaxed. I felt, "She's really seen something today." We lingered in the silence until our session was over.

Living in Well-Being and Love

When we're seeing and honoring where "seeing" comes from, the next step is living there more of the time. The simple gift of living in well-being is that not only do we benefit from this enriching experience, it also awakens others to their true nature.

People feel the calmness, the serenity, the courage to live well without necessarily having much in the material sense; they feel the love, the well-being that emanates from within us. Their true nature responds, because that is everyone's birthright, whether they know it or not.

I had the honor and privilege of being invited by a client to offer a few webinars to the group she was working with in Greenland. They had some background in this understanding, and had experienced a degree of their own well-being. Most of them had not met me online, although some were aware of my story; that I knew Syd before he had his experience, and so on. There was an immediate connection when we saw each other on the screen, looking at each other with interest, and with a feeling of respect and gratitude for each other.

Their Inuit culture is very deep, very spiritually oriented. They felt me spiritually, more than heard my words. They called me Grandmother, which was an honor. I've been called Mama. I've been called Grandma. I've been called other names in the

Mentored by Mind

early days. . . those I won't mention. . .   So, Mama and Grandmother is really beautiful to me. I love that.

Our sessions were so rich and enlightening. They loved my stories of Syd, how an ordinary working man had such a spontaneous epiphany that completely transformed his life, and gave the mental health field a new paradigm of health rather than looking at dysfunction.

They were fascinated that Syd never had any training in talking with an audience, that he used to be terrified of speaking publicly, yet with this new inner enlightenment he began to teach mental health professionals, and soon began to travel the world, sharing the spiritual gifts he'd uncovered.

They had deep respect that a University in the United States had started a new innate mental health department to share Syd's teachings for several years, before closing, at Syd's request. He realized that the teachings were creating some difficulties within the traditional psychology department, and respected their separate realities. He knew the teachings would never be lost; however, he didn't want to make anyone uncomfortable.

These stories gave the Inuit group hope; it evoked possibility in them. If an ordinary man like Syd could have such a profound experience without seeking or knowing anything about the fundamental Principles that all humans have to create their experience, then they felt what Syd found was open to them as well.

Even people who know nothing about the Principles, feel love. Like the people I met online for a webinar from Costa Rica. When they were first introduced to me, they wondered, who is this woman? They didn't understand me at first, even with a translator, because what I was saying was so foreign to them, even translated into Spanish.

Sometimes when you have a translator, it can be difficult, pausing in the flow of what you're saying so the translator can keep up with you. What I really count on during those translations is that the feeling between me and the translator is very strong, and that we are deeply in harmony, and very committed to the message. Because ultimately, it's the feeling that will touch people, not the words.

A couple of days after the webinar, I spoke with Alexandra, my client in Costa Rica and with Ana, the translator, who lives in the USA. Alexandra wanted to let me know that she showed the webinar to a number of her colleagues and friends, who hadn't been able to attend. The key things they said, when Alexandra asked them what they heard on the recording, was that they felt me. They felt the love. They didn't really know what I was talking about, but it was the feeling that attracted them to sign up for the retreat I'd be doing there. I'll

Mentored by Mind

say it again: They felt the love. Love transcends time and space, love transcends language.

A man from Greece was on that webinar; he was very moved by the sharing. He understood both English and Spanish because he had lived in South America for a number of years. At one point toward the end, he was very emotional and complimentary about the feeling that he felt was coming from me.

I thanked him, then let him know that feeling was coming from him. That it was his feeling he was experiencing. He thought it was me, but it was him. Now, I won't dismiss that our feeling can be a catalyst, can be the spark to ignite another's deep feeling; however, ultimately, it is the person's true nature that has awoken.

Our True Nature is our Angel

When we really embrace that deep feeling of well-being, we're honestly embracing our own true nature, our own angel. Unknowingly, that's what people feel—they feel their angel.

I can't tell you how important that is. I had a businesswoman come to the island for a private four-day program. It was one of the most beautiful times I'd ever had mentoring. The woman, Leticia, was very intrigued about angels; she felt she had angels in her life and honored their presence. They were outside of her, she told me, but she felt guided by them.

I listened deeply and said very little to her on the first day, just hanging out, learning about her and her family. Then we listened to one of Syd's tapes at the end. I wasn't sure what to do about the angel stories so I trusted that wisdom would guide me, and had a great night's sleep.

The second day Leticia opened up even more about being guided by angels. What came out of me spontaneously was to ask her gently to consider that she was the angel. I suggested she not give her spiritual power away, and to cut out the middle man, to honor her inner angel, her Higher Self. I suggested that if she could just consider this, it would change her life. I knew she was very tied into the long-held belief about angels guiding her, and I wanted her to be able to connect her

Mentored by Mind

feeling of angels guiding her, to the fact that, her Higher Self was/is guiding her.

And in an instant, she got that. She really got that. "I feel the truth of what you're saying, Elsie. I love what you said about not giving up my spiritual power, and cutting out the middle man—or middle woman, in this case." She grinned, stood up, and gave me a big hug. "I never realized that I'm my own angel. That feels so right. I don't feel I'm losing anything. I feel like I've gained a friend—myself! I had no idea that I could be my best friend and mentor."

That was a huge insight for Leticia; to recognize and honor her own true nature. Her life changed, once she connected more deeply to herSelf. Her insight opened the door to "seeing" that she, and all of us, are consistently being mentored by Mind; that in reality, we're being mentored by our Higher Selves.

Even when we have that ping pong ball going back and forth, the intellect saying "Oh, I did this, I should have known better," then wisdom saying "So what? Now you 'see' where it comes from." And you can watch the ping pong ball go back and forth, and soon it's only one ball, and then there's no ball, and you are home.

Listening and Sharing in Shorthand

Deep listening is a shorthand way of being guided by wisdom. Deep listening is the quality of listening without anything on your mind; of listening without expectations, of NOT listening for wisdom. Listening is stillness in action.

In the previous story, not knowing how to mentor Leticia, I listened deeply. And wisdom guided. Deep listening opened the door for me to work in a new area that I never dreamed I'd work in: Juvenile Justice.

When the Deputy Director of Juvenile Justice first called and invited me to provide a 3-day seminar for the department, I turned her down. Having never worked in this area, I felt insecure, and recommended she contact a colleague of mine who was familiar with youth corrections.

The Director said, "Well, your colleague suggested we contact you!" That statement gave me pause, so I listened. As I heard their need, I began to feel interest, and as the call ended, it came to me to suggest we have a group call, with a cross section of the department joining us.

Long story short, I worked with this team for a couple of years. It was one of the most memorable projects I've undertaken.

Mentored by Mind

When I was brought in to work with the director, counselors, probation officers, and administration, I learned that the traditional approach they were using was based on behavior modification. As I listened to them describe what programs they were doing, I could see some common ground, and I could also see the stress they felt in their attachment to youth's behavior changing and remaining consistent. They were very keen on reducing recidivism and had tried many other programs without achieving reliable results.

The first thing I introduced them to was a simple explanation of the Principles. Then I focused on helping them recognize their own innate wisdom. The perfect example occurred during a break, when I was speaking with Carlos, a probation officer. I asked him how he had enjoyed the first session. His response was, "I'm confused, Elsie. I get a feeling for Mind, as I have a religious background, and I feel you're pointing to God. And I resonated with the Principle of Thought, as you described it. But I don't get Consciousness at all."

I listened intently, then asked Carlos why he'd become a probation officer. I was curious to know what drew him to this line of work.

Carlos paused for a moment before replying. "As a teenager, I was in a gang. I saw some of my homies killed, and I saw others addicted, and to support their addictions, committing crimes that landed them in jail. I realized I didn't want to end up like they did. So I decided to become a probation officer working with kids. I felt I could really relate to where they are coming from because of my past experiences."

A deep feeling of connection happened between us. Carlos had shared something powerful with me, and we both felt it. What I saw in his sharing was that he had "realized" he didn't want to end up as some of his friends had.

I said to him, "Carlos, you said you realized you didn't want to end up as your buddies did. Do you know what "realized" means in the Three Principles?"

"Haven't a clue."

"It means Consciousness. You had a moment of insight, of deep awareness, and I would say that changed your life."

Carlos's face lit up. "You're kidding! For real? You mean I was using Consciousness and didn't know it?"

"For real, Carlos. That's how simple the Principles are. They're working for you already, as they are for all of humanity, whether we know it or not."

I asked Carlos if he'd be willing to share his realization with the group after the break, and he beamed. "I'd be happy to."

Mentored by Mind

Carlos's sharing brought a new perspective to the group. One of their own had a moment of realization. Because his feeling was so strong as he shared, the group sensed there was something worthwhile happening, and they paid more attention as the day went on.

The second thing I focused on was how to "see" and speak to the innate health in the youth. Drawing out the kids' wisdom rather than pointing to their dysfunction, as a means of correcting behavior, was a completely new paradigm for them to consider.

However, because of Carlos sharing his story, the staff started to ponder that this new paradigm might work. Insights started to pop within the group, and I heard comments like, "Wow, okay, yah, I'm starting to feel my wisdom"; "I had an insight!"; "There must be something to this."

With this learning simmering in their consciousness, their engagement with the children changed, in the most natural way. It was as if they had different eyes with which to see, and they started to look at the kids' wisdom, rather than their behavior. And the children's behavior began to change.

Although I worked primarily with the adults, there were a few times where I was brought in to work with the youth. The staff had already been working with them so they had a tiny bit of understanding, mainly about their innate mental health.

Elsie Spittle

The kids were finding this hard to believe. After all, they'd been pointed, innocently, to their poor behavior for so long, the idea they could possibly have a natural goodness within was very hard to take in.

It was in my first session with a group of young boys that I first experienced speaking in, and honoring shorthand. A young lad who must have been 12 or so, shared his thoughts with me. "Miss Elsie, I just don't know about this innate health stuff. It sounds like a lot of hooey to me."

I continued to listen. He said "There was a minute or so where I did feel like a little bit of calm, but then I got angry at one of the other kids, because he said something bad about my Mom, and so I threw a chair at him. After that, they put me in the quiet room, so there's no way I have this wisdom you're talking about. I wouldn't have done what I did if I had this wisdom."

He was so ticked off at himself, so at a loss, my heart went out to him. I wanted to cuddle him, which wasn't allowed. What I heard, in the stillness of my listening, was that he had one minute of calm, of quiet. He'd had an experience of that one minute, and I latched onto it and wouldn't let it go. I continued to briefly say, "You had a minute of calm."

And he'd come back with, "Yes, but..." and I'd go back to "You had one minute." It was like a game of ping pong, until

Mentored by Mind

finally he paused. I think he just got tired of me not letting go and he went still. And I stopped. And then there was just quiet. And that quiet told me: he knows. He got a glimmer of knowing, and I knew he'd be okay. My eyes fill with tears as I write this. Knowing is such a precious gift, never to be forgotten.

It doesn't matter if this boy's experience was only a minute. When Syd had his enlightenment experience, as he often said publicly at his conferences and in his recordings, it lasted maybe four or five seconds. That blows my mind! Look at what those few timeless seconds uncovered in this welder, and for the world.

The Quiet is the Gold

A minute is like an eternity. At a retreat in Norway, I shared the story of the young lad who'd experienced that powerful moment of calm. Among the audience were some educators, including a teacher who worked with "at risk" youth in her school. The teacher, Maja, said, "Elsie, that's usually when I dive in. When I'm working with at risk youth, and if they get quiet, that's when I feel, okay now, I can really jump in and start to teach. And yet you're saying just be quiet at that point? Be still, they've got it?"

"Yes, that's exactly what I'm saying. The quiet is the gold; the quiet has the power to stir another's wisdom so they become their own teacher. In other words, the quiet can be the teacher, as well as the gold."

The audience was still, absorbing this conversation between Maja and me. It was a comfortable silence so I let it ride.

Then Maja said "What you're saying feels right; it resonates for me, but that's really new." And I left her in that feeling of resonance. I didn't carry on and teach any more, because I knew she got it.

I turned to the audience and said, "I'm curious about what you're seeing about the quiet. When you've been working with

Mentored by Mind

clients and you may have experienced a moment of quiet, what happens for you? Yes, Morten?"

Morten: "Since you've been talking about this, I think that's something that I've always done; is to try to stop and leave the space. But I've been noticing it more. I don't really have a whole lot to say about it, except that I totally feel what you're feeling, and to be able to watch the client ponder, and let it sink in, and then see what they come up with—it's cool."

Elsie: "I love that! Often times, Morten, when Syd would be with us as a group, or even individually, he wouldn't say, *"Okay, you've had a moment of quiet now, I'm not going to say anything else, this is a teaching moment."*

Syd didn't teach that way. He taught by demonstration. It was in those moments when he could see our furrowed brows start to ease, and our faces light up, then he'd say, *"Okay, let's have a break now. Let's go to lunch. Or just talk amongst yourselves."*

Maja: "Ya, I was just talking with a client this morning and she was really pondering the idea of looking within herself for her own satisfaction. And then she started to get really intellectual, like wanting to understand it, and it felt really good to say, 'Let's stop. We can talk about it more next time, but don't think so hard about it.'"

Elsie Spittle

Elsie: "Good for you, Maja, that's excellent; so respectful, in helping your client slip out of using her thinking against herself, trying to figure it out, and getting stressed in the process.

"It reminds me of a quote of Syd's: *'It's not that we have two minds; we have Mind and we can use in two different ways.'* I used to think we had two minds; Wisdom mind and the intellectual mind, and they were two separate things. At one point, I finally got a glimmer of what Syd had said and I felt empowered. I felt empowered to use Mind as it's meant to be used. Why would I use Mind to think negative thoughts? It would be like banging my head against the wall. I know we all do that sometimes; that's part of human nature. Then, if we're lucky, we wake up, and realize—"Wow, that hurts! Banging my head against the wall isn't serving me well.'"

Maja: "Sometimes the banging is what wakes us up, I think."

I had to chuckle at that, as did the audience, and the laughter lightened the feeling in the room. "Well, that's true. It's like sticking your finger in the electric socket, and you get a shock, and you go, 'Whoa, enough of that.'"

Maja: "Well, I know I can feel it more than I can think it."

It's a Feeling World

Yes, it's definitely a feeling world brought about by our thinking. We are thinking beings with the gift of feelings as our guidance system. Feelings are wisdom's way of telling us if we're heading in the right direction or not. The more we slip into our wisdom, the more we are guided by Mind, where wisdom resides.

I'll give you an example. Amanda is a client who is doing incredible work as a coach for a variety of groups and individuals. She said to me the other day on our call that she'd come to a crux in the next stage of her work. She was struggling with trying to figure out what the next step was, brooding about, "Should I do this, or should I do that?" She really didn't know what to do next.

Then Amanda said, "I went out for a walk and I just said, okay, Mind, tell me what to do." I listened quietly as she spoke and heard her say, two or three times, "Okay, Mind, tell me what to do."

There was something about that statement that didn't feel quite right to me. It didn't land. And then it came to me; I didn't think about it, it just came out, and I said "You know, Amanda, I suggest you don't ask Mind—ask yourSELF."

Amanda looked puzzled and I could see that she was separating Mind from herself, as if there was/is a duality. I

Elsie Spittle

repeated, "Ask yourself, Amanda, because you are part of Mind."

I paused as something new occurred to me. "I'll go deeper, and suggest that you don't ask; just be and the answer will come. When we start to realize more fully that we are Mind, and that logic strikes a chord, that resonance means we're beginning to see that if we're part of mind, then we are Mind; there is no separation. This realization is very empowering."

"I'm not really getting this, Elsie, although I sense the Truth of what you're saying. I've got to figure it out; I'm Mind, so Mind should be able to tell me what to do, and I would like to know now."

Her earnest declaration that she wanted to know what Mind had to say 'now' brought a smile to my face and I said, "You're a love, Amanda. I really respect that you want to know 'now.' That's a very natural human desire; to know now. Waiting to know is not usually an easy attribute for us humans."

I lingered for a moment of quiet, then said, "Can you consider being comfortable with not knowing?" Amanda shook her head, "I don't know, Elsie. Patience is not my strong suit."

"You're very honest, Amanda. I honor that quality in you."

My mind went still for a few moments, then I said, "Let me ask you this. What if 'not knowing' moves into 'just living'?

Mentored by Mind

Just living is a state of mind where you're not harboring thoughts like 'I don't know; I'm so impatient; I wish I could be comfortable in not knowing.' What if you let those thought just slip away, and instead you're thinking ordinary relaxing thoughts like, 'I'm going to scramble some eggs for lunch, or I'm going to go for a walk, or I'm going shopping.'

"When you let those 'not knowing' thoughts slip away, then you're not bothered when you don't know the next step. Your trust in Mind becomes so inherent that your natural patience is released, and you just live, knowing the answer will come in time—not necessarily in your time—it will be in Mind's time."

Once again, I repeated, "Don't ask, just be."

There was a lengthy silence as Amanda reflected on what I'd shared.

Then I asked, "Amanda, how is this conversation sitting with you?"

"I had different thoughts as you were talking. I was just reflecting back on this morning before our call, when I was feeling all entangled in a lot of thinking. And I realized that as I've gotten a little more grounded in this understanding, what's starting to happen is, when I see myself going to that state of impatience, and it feels like it's going to sweep me off my feet, I'm just going to wait it out.

Elsie Spittle

"I think what you talked about, Elsie, in honoring our wisdom, really spoke to me because this is what I glimpsed right now in my life. I'm beginning to see that when I'm feeling like I'm not really understanding, if I take my mind off my personal thinking, the answer will occur to me in time."

Amanda continued, "The possibility of seeing things differently when I'm not caught up in my thinking is an opportunity for seeing things from a different perspective, and is very, very hopeful to me. There were a few moments when you were talking, where I felt that just honoring that possibility really landed for me. Honoring our wisdom more, and seeing how that extends into honoring ourselves more as an embodiment of that wisdom."

Amanda's words went right to my soul. "Oh my, I love your original voice, Amanda. I love your phrase 'wait out'; when you don't know what to do next, you'll just wait it out. And I felt your calmness as you were sharing that. Even though you say you were entangled in your personal thinking earlier this morning, the way you're coming across now, I feel your 'waiting it out' calmness. And I love what you said about the embodiment of our body…say that again…"

"When you said, 'honor your wisdom,' Elsie, I see that honoring our wisdom becomes an extension of honoring ourselves, as an embodiment of that wisdom."

Mentored by Mind

"That's absolutely beautiful, Amanda; thank you so much for sharing."

"Another thing that really impacted me," Amanda said, "was when you said those words 'just be.' I felt so much relief; it was like a light went off as an opportunity to really embrace the opportunity to just live. Then I saw how being in the discomfort of the unknown, rather than trusting the answer will come, is taking me out of enjoying my life.

"It reminds me of the old saying about, 'Jesus take the wheel.' It's kind of like, 'Mind take the wheel' and I realized that we can have the wheel back, at any time, because we're Mind. Now I see that I've been missing life, and the opportunity to be more present, and to let Mind take the wheel, and I'm part of Mind."

"That's so powerful, Amanda. You're talking in shorthand. Those phrases, 'take the wheel,' and what came out when I was talking with you at the start of our conversation, about 'Don't ask, just be,' is shorthand. It's like those phrases are an embodiment of Mind; of Mind speaking, because Mind doesn't have to say much. Those shorthand phrases illustrate that it's a 'feeling world,' where the feeling is beyond the words, and the feeling brings understanding.

"As an example, I'll share how Syd often taught us without words. Over the years, there were many times when he

Elsie Spittle

wouldn't even say anything, where his teaching would be contained in a look. I might be babbling about something where I was wanting an answer from him, and he would just look at me with a penetrating, calm look.

"That look had the power to stop me; it would stop my intellect grappling for an answer. That look would settle me down, and before too long, the answer would come from within. And the answer usually was, 'Be still. Just live.' This is sharing in shorthand, Amanda."

Amanda gave a great sigh and I could see she was full to the brim with her new insights. "To wrap up our session, I can see that now you're uncovering your wisdom you'll take the wheel more and more of the time, just as you did during our conversation, Amanda. And you'll find more peace and enjoyment in your life and work."

"Thank you, Elsie. I feel very moved and I look forward to our next conversation."

Honor What You Do Know

Amanda and I had a follow-up session a couple of weeks later. As she appeared on the computer screen, I could see that her face was drawn and she looked tired. After we exchanged greetings, I asked her how she was doing and if there was anything she wanted to explore.

"The last couple of days I've been in a lot of self doubt thinking," Amanda began. "It's so interesting, because I've been noticing this myself, and realizing how my reality reflects my thinking. I'm kind of believing my thinking, and then believing my reality, but it's curious, because I'm getting a sense that my thinking is my illusion. I don't know if that makes sense, Elsie?"

"Tell me more, Amanda."

Amanda was still as she gathered her thoughts, then slowly began, "I'm noticing how much I start trying to rely on something external to give me relief from my thinking. And so, it was interesting joining our call today because, suddenly, I had the feeling of not remembering anything intellectually about the 3 P's. It's like I've forgotten everything.

"At the end of our last call, Elsie, as I listened to you speak, I started to have the feeling where, as a child, your Grandma puts her arms around you and holds your close, and you feel this sense of relief and love.

Elsie Spittle

"And I was having that feeling with you, yet in the back of my mind, I was thinking I need to find a way to remember to just let go of the steering wheel. The problem is, in the middle of stress, how do you remember to take your hands off the steering wheel?

"And then I had the insight, that actually, we simply need to trust that wisdom will show up, when it needs to show up. So, it's not that we clutch onto the need to remember to let go of the wheel, like a technique or something; it's just trusting that letting go will happen at the right time. That there's nothing in us that's broken; it just will happen, even the letting go will happen at the right time."

Amanda's face had brightened as she shared her insights. No longer was she looking stressed; and her tone had become calmer and her words slower.

"That's really well said, Amanda! Threaded throughout what you were sharing, I hear you referring to illusion. And you even end your sharing by referring to the illusionary nature of thought; how reality changes according to our thinking in the moment. To have a glimmer of the illusionary nature of life is very profound.

"That insight is so meaningful, Amanda. I honor what you do know. I don't care about what you don't know."

"Excuse me, Elsie; what did you say?"

Mentored by Mind

"I said that I don't care about what you don't know."

"Could you explain that a bit more, Elsie. You've lost me. I thought it was important to investigate what we don't know so we can move forward."

"Okay, let me put it this way. Your question reminds me of one of our earlier sessions, when I spoke about honoring what we do know, rather than honoring the dip in our understanding, like when we dip low into our entangled thinking.

"For example, when you realized that letting go is not a technique, and that your wisdom will show up when needed, you honored your wisdom, rather than dwelling on your personal thoughts. And that elevated your understanding, and your reality. Are you with me?"

"Yes, go on."

"As a matter of fact, you already had a shift in consciousness, because noticing that you were trying to change your state of mind by external means points to you being at a higher level at that moment in time. That's profound; that's the blessing of wisdom."

"Amanda, I hear your wisdom woven throughout your sharing. You had a glimmer that reality is illusionary. You had a glimmer that letting go isn't a technique. You honored your wisdom. The shift in your understanding is huge."

Amanda's face was glowing, and she wiped a tear from her eye.

"The last thing I want to say is that the deep feeling you're experiencing now is your true nature, expressing itself as wisdom. This means that your inner Self has woken up more, and that's why you don't have to remember—because your wisdom is more readily available now.

"It doesn't matter if we cover wisdom up. I also cover up my true nature sometimes with my thinking. And so what? The gift is that I'm mostly aware that I'm doing it, and I know wisdom is always available, just as you do, Amanda. That knowing helps me to relax and just 'be.'

"I'm going to wrap it up now, Amanda, and I'd love for you to just sit quietly after you log off the screen, and rest in the beauty of your insights. I'm very moved by what you shared. I feel we've had a soul-to-soul conversation. We felt each other's essence, and that was so enriching. I honor and thank you."

Part Three

"Seeing" and Standing in Truth

Insight is such a precious gift—a gift that keeps giving. I continue to find the truth in that spiritual fact. As I was reflecting on that this morning, I recalled an online group session I had facilitated, where several people talked about connection. They felt insight was a deeper connection to Mind, to wisdom, and I completely agree.

Others talked about being able to "see" beyond their thinking, and in doing so, had gained insight into that deeper connection to Mind. I was really moved by the purity of the response from the group. However, the group didn't quite see how wise they were. It's true that sometimes we don't see our own wisdom. It takes our intellect longer to catch up with insight, so often there is a gap between insight and intellect.

I felt moved to encourage the group to pause for a moment and consider the words and the understanding they had shared with each other, and with me, on that call. I also encouraged them to listen to the recording later, letting them know that the truth they had shared might surprise them and have even deeper meaning for them when they listened again. The deeper meaning is evidence that points to insight continuing to blossom; even the same insight has the capacity to blossom again and again.

I've been asked, "How do we know that what we're seeing is true?" Occasionally, we may wonder if what we're seeing is

Elsie Spittle

our personal truth. Is truth subjective? Is it objective? Can we trust what we're seeing?

In response to those questions, I always come back to the feeling—the feeling of our "seeing." Everything circles back to the feeling. Why? Because the feeling is the expression of our true nature. The feeling is coming from wisdom. And that feeling is what will guide us to knowing whether we're seeing with our personal thinking or with Universal Mind.

An example came to mind to share with the group; an interesting experience of "seeing" and standing in truth. I'd been talking with Ian, and his wife, Evelyn, who had gone through some very serious health issues over the last few months. Then came a point of recovery in Evelyn's health and well being, which brought them hope and inspiration that the healing would continue.

Each time I talked with this couple I was struck by their wisdom, and the strength of her recovery. Even though it was Evelyn who had these physical challenges, Ian was also facing issues, as Evelyn's caregiver.

I could see Evelyn and Ian's faces change as we talked, and realized they both were growing from the inside-out. Even though Evelyn wasn't as talkative as she had been in the past, the depth of feeling she had reached in her spiritual evolution

Mentored by Mind

was tangible. I observed the same evolution happening with Ian.

The last time I spoke with them I was so moved by their journey that I suggested, if they felt comfortable, they might want to share their story at a retreat we were mutually facilitating.

Prior to my suggestion, they'd kept their health journey private. They weren't sharing it, other than with family and close friends. I let them know how touched I was by their courage, and that their story could help and inspire others who were going through similar situations.

Ian and Evelyn rose to the occasion, and they shared their experience at the retreat. It was very moving. People were in tears as they were inspired and became hopeful, seeing a new way to honor our bodies, the vessel of our spiritual nature.

Participants got a deep glimmer of seeing how our spiritual nature can help us through very challenging times. Doctors had told the couple that Evelyn might not recover from her physical frailties, and for them not to expect too much. They both intuitively knew not to focus on that. They didn't challenge the doctors; they were very respectful. They just continued on their journey with hope—and were open to possibilities.

Elsie Spittle

Now we come to another milestone. The second day was similar, with people asking the couple to carry on with their story of recovery, and so on. I was one of the facilitators, so I let this theme continue. On the third day of the retreat, people kept asking Ian and Evelyn to tell them more about their experience. They said, "We can see you both have gone deeper, and we love what you're saying. Tell us more about what it was like for you."

Finally, it dawned on me that people were focusing more on the couple's journey than on their own. In innocence, the participants were missing the plot, as I had been. The retreat became all about this couple and their story of courage, hope, inspiration, and possibilities; however, what about them? What about the participants' journeys?

As I became aware that the questions kept coming back to the couple's experience, I wasn't sure what to do with this situation. I "saw" it but didn't know what to do. During the break, I spoke to Ian and Evelyn, and let them know what I was seeing. Within moments, they said, "Yes, absolutely; we're seeing this too."

The three of us still weren't sure what to do. We were in the unknown. Ian, Evelyn, and me, as the senior lady, the grandma, were "seeing" and not knowing what to do with that seeing.

Mentored by Mind

The only thing I knew was that what was happening in the retreat needed attention. I didn't know how that would unfold. And then it came to me. I was moved to talk with someone in the audience, and I asked her what she would like to hear? I asked her what she thought would be of interest to the group?

And this beautiful soul responded with pure truth. I knew her words were dead on. She said, "I'd like to hear more about Syd's core message, and I feel the group would benefit from this as well."

The light came on, and Mind guided. Everything came out when we got back together again. I was able to gently, diplomatically, and firmly, point people back to their own "being." I asked the group not to lose sight of their own journey, of their own strength, courage, and most importantly, their own soul. Ian and Evelyn also spoke up and encouraged the group to look inside themselves, rather than focusing on the couple's journey.

It was an amazing turn around. As we shared what we were seeing, standing in truth and integrity, the audience went with it. The audience felt the truth of what we were saying, and a beautiful space was born. We had come full circle, from honoring a couple's spiritual journey to honoring our Universal journey.

Elsie Spittle

We sometimes get so drawn in and enamored with someone else's journey, we forget to honor our own. That is how innocent we are. We forget to honor the core message from Syd; that we all have this strength, courage, purity, and wisdom inside us. The more we honor that, the more we stand in truth, the more we evolve, and the less words we need. We come back to sharing in shorthand—less words, deeper feeling.

That was such a powerful experience. It's still blossoming for me. When I spoke with this couple the other day, they informed me that experience is continuing to blossom for them too. Evelyn and Ian are seeing how fewer words have more power. They're seeing that it's a beautiful gift, standing in the integrity of what we "see."

After the morning session with the group, I was invited to lunch by a colleague who was at the retreat. John said to me, "You know, not everybody could do what you did. You shared what you saw with gentleness, and with directness. The words you said didn't come out scolding; you weren't scolding the group. You weren't saying, 'No, no, don't pay so much attention to Evelyn and Ian.' You just said, 'come back to your own true self'."

"John, isn't it wonderful that this ability to guide with strength and gentleness is something that is available to everyone, in whatever situation appears in their lives? I love that."

Mentored by Mind

John was really taken by how you can stand in truth and say what needs to be said, whether it's popular or not. And he loved that Ian and Evelyn stood in integrity and took the focus off themselves, and pointed people back to their true nature.

It struck me that when you are present in pure wisdom, you know how to do what needs to be done, without thinking about "how to." It's back to the famous quote of Syd's, *"doing without doing."*

Share Clearly and with Love

As I write this, I'm reminded of a time when I was consulting and training in the corporate world on the Three Principles. There were times when, with rapport, love and understanding, I was able to share something that wasn't necessarily pleasant for a manager or a CEO to hear.

Often, I would be brought in to interview a cross section of employees to get a sense of how the executive team could enhance their relationships with their workers. This particular organization I was invited into had low morale problems that resulted in rework in their product which, of course, affected their bottom line. Safety issues and accidents were prevalent, and sick pay was going through the roof; again, resulting in lower financials.

At the start of my interviews, some of the workers were appreciative that their bosses were taking the time to have me interview them. Among others there was a lack of trust that the leaders would do anything with the information I was gathering. I did my best to set aside their skepticism, and let them know I felt this was truly an opportunity for a step level change in the culture of the organization. The feeling of trust that I had for the plant manager came across and did settle some employees, but not all.

Sometimes the feedback offered by the workforce about their bosses could be tinged with anger and resentment; other times, workers had deep concerns about the safety of the environment they worked in. I listened attentively and respectfully. I didn't try to change anyone's mind; I stayed as neutral as possible.

Once I gathered my information, and reflected on it, I prepared a report and shared what I had observed with the executive team, offering positive feedback at the beginning, in terms of the employees appreciating that the leaders gave me time to interview them.

I shared what I saw because that was my job, and I was moved by wisdom and Mind to do so, in as pertinent and blame free manner as I could. I was comfortable and strong in knowing that what I was seeing was true. I didn't feel any attachment to the outcome, and was not concerned about keeping my job if the plant manager didn't like my report. I had worked with the plant manager prior to being brought into the organization, and our rapport was very good.

However, I knew it was up to the plant manager and the executive team to "hear" the report with open hearts and open minds. My job was to interview with respect, listen deeply, and remain neutral to the information I gathered. To simply "see"' the information as that; information, not an indictment, to present the report to the leaders without judgment, and to continue listening for wisdom to guide me during this process.

Elsie Spittle

I repeat: Whether people "hear" the truth or not, is up to them. As trainers/ coaches/mentors, our job, as I see it, is first, and foremost, to listen; then to share as clearly and purely as we can. The groups' or individuals' job is to "hear and see."

Knowing this is very helpful, because, in a positive sense, it takes the responsibility off us to "fix" people. Knowing this prompts us to offer those we're speaking with an opportunity to embrace their own innate "listening and hearing" capacities.

I suspect each of us has had times when we've shared something with a client or group, and if they haven't heard what we're offering, we may have felt responsible. And I'm not saying that sometimes we may not be responsible, in terms of not being present to the groups' needs, or listening deeply enough.

Typically, we end up judging and blaming ourselves. Sometimes, in our frustration, we may blame the group. We may think they weren't ready; they're closed minded; and so on.

When we see that our job is to share truth as best we can, and our clients' job is to hear or not, it relieves us of intellectual responsibility. "Seeing" moves us toward more faith and trust—in life, and in business. "Seeing" is a wonderful way to serve, adding to productivity and improving the bottom line, with integrity.

"Seeing" the Beauty Beyond Behavior

I spoke with a woman yesterday in Kenya, who was inquiring about my mentoring. Although I was booked, I was so drawn by her previous email and the work she's doing, amid the many challenges she faces in her workplace environment, I was moved to offer her a call.

Victoria works with abused women and children, and some of the stories that she shared with me are horrendous. What these children and women are going through is unbelievable, and she said that some of the men are also being abused by other men.

Although the stories Victoria shared were heartbreaking, it was a powerful conversation. I learned so much from her. I've worked in disenfranchised communities where there's so much pain and suffering. Many of the residents feel hopeless, and try to cover their pain with drugs and alcohol, then commit crimes to support their addictions.

What I heard from Victoria about the conditions she's working in really went beyond my experience. What struck me so deeply was her level of calmness and compassion. The way she pours her heart and soul into working with these beautiful souls is extraordinary. She sees the behavior and what's happening, yet she sees beyond that, to their beautiful souls. That's how she talks about these individuals.

Elsie Spittle

Victoria said, "The reason I've reached out to you is because of a young boy I've never met. Kwame is in my community and he's gone through such horrific experiences. He's nine years old!" After hearing what had happened to this young lad, Victoria was deeply moved to help him. She said, "I see he's not broken, despite what's happened to him, but I don't know what to do."

As she shared Kwame's story with me, I kept hearing her love and compassion. I knew that if she met this boy, coming from that deep feeling of love, she would automatically be helping him.

As I was listening to Victoria describe what had happened to Kwame, honest to God, I felt my arms move into a circle as if I could cuddle him to me. My heart went out to him so much, as Victoria's had.

Kwame had become a drug runner at the age of nine, forced to become a slave because of a situation he was involved in. He'd been in an accident through no fault of his own, where another child had died, yet the community saw him at fault, and punished him in extreme measures.

And so Victoria asked me, "How can I help him?" It was obvious to me that her love for this child was the best help possible. I pointed her back to her wisdom. As we spoke, it started to come clear to her that she already was living in

Mentored by Mind

knowing "how to help." This was very reassuring to her. It was so simple that it bypassed her intellect's "how to" question. She realized the power of just meeting a lost soul with love, and knowing that, in that soul-to-soul connection, Mind will guide.

Then Victoria said another thing that sparked for me. She'd not had any formal training in the Principles. She isn't a counselor or a therapist so she was helping people informally. Victoria began to get an uneasy feeling that the work she was doing wasn't really helping anymore. She wondered, "Now what?"

Out of the blue, a book about the Principles arrived for her in the mail. It changed her life. Just that book. Not meeting anyone, not knowing if there was anybody else in Kenya working with the 3 Principles.

Victoria went online and started to see all the resources available, somehow found me as well, and reached out to me. She found Syd's materials and began listening to his recordings and reading his books, and her wisdom began to flourish.

Victoria's friends and colleagues noticed the change in her, and sometimes she shared what she'd learned with them. Other times, she'd just be with them in her true "identity," not realizing that her newly calm presence was helping them. And they wanted to learn more.

Elsie Spittle

In her innocence, she didn't see that one's calm presence can influence others. She asked me, "How do I help my friends, Elsie?" I had to chuckle; she's such an innocent soul.

I said to Victoria, "You're already doing it! Just keep coming from your true nature, and you'll know how."

One of Victoria's friends is a very religious person. In conversation, her friend, Annika, revealed to Victoria that she felt she had been so broken, she'd lost all hope, until she found Jesus. Annika felt Jesus was saving her through her born-again faith.

Victoria said to her friend, "Annika, you're not broken. Nobody is broken. We're all whole inside, in our true nature." And the woman went away very thoughtful. A few days later, Annika got frightened about what she'd heard from Victoria, about not being broken. She "heard" it, but it scared her.

I know that feeling. I know, because that happened to me, upon hearing Syd. I heard him, and asked him not to talk to me about this "Principles nonsense." That's what happened to Victoria's friend, Annika. She said to Victoria, "I feel like I've lost my faith, so don't talk to me any more about not being broken. I feel like I've lost my faith, and I don't need Jesus to heal me anymore." Annika was absolutely frightened out of her wits.

And her dear friend, Victoria, knew exactly what was going on. Victoria told Annika, with great gentleness, "I don't

Mentored by Mind

see that you've lost your faith; it's just another way of looking at your faith. It feels to me like you're seeing the page before the words."

Victoria's words hit me like a bolt of lightening. "You're seeing the page before the words." Her friend was still very disconcerted by this. And Victoria knew enough to just be silent, and to let Annika rest her mind, so they had a cup of tea together.

Isn't that beautiful? I was so taken by Victoria's natural wisdom that had been released from within, simply by reading Syd's books; they had touched her so deeply. Victoria has awakened to her true nature, and she knows "how to" even though in her innocence, she didn't realize she was doing the perfect thing—sharing in the most perfect way. Knowing when to share, and when to be still. Such is the power and perfect guidance of our true identity.

Note: I wanted to update you on Victoria's story. Kwame is now living in a home that specializes in children with trauma. The best news is that he is away from his community, which would never let him forget the label they had given him. So in a way he gets a fresh start.

Victoria's friend, Annika, is an insatiable 3 Principles student and her marriage, which was very shaky, has had fresh life breathed into it due to her understanding.

Feeling the Feeling more than the Words

Another story comes to mind that a client shared with me during our session. As you may have gathered by now, I like to tell stories, as stories contain inspiration and results. One of Syd's main teaching points was telling stories about how people had transformed their lives, and in doing so, helped others transform theirs. He intuitively knew that insightful stories have the deep feeling and power to awaken other souls.

I was still resonating from my conversation with Victoria, when I had another call scheduled with Samantha. After sharing a bit of Victoria's story with her, changing Victoria's name and location to ensure privacy, I asked Sam if anything lit up for her.

Sam: "Elsie, I'd love to tell you a story that kind of blew me away. It is similar to Victoria's story, although it is about a family member. I have an older sister who has struggled with very severe anxiety and alcoholism. She's really been lost. I've been around the Principles for almost 20 years now, and throughout that time, I've only shared if she's asked; mostly I've just tried to be there for her and to love her.

"Once in a while, I got the feeling that she was resonating with what I expressed to her, but mostly she was very closed minded. Then, a couple of months ago, she was having a really difficult time, and she reached out to me."

Mentored by Mind

Sam's voice started to waiver, and she paused for a moment to compose herself. "For the first time, she seemed more vulnerable, and asked me what I was seeing that had led to the change in my life. So, the door was open.

"I have no idea what I said. Whatever I shared came from my wisdom, and the fact that I saw beyond her behavior to her wholeness, and I felt like I spoke to her wholeness. Three days later, inexplicably, my sister again reached out to me, and told me that she saw she wasn't broken."

Once again, Sam's voice quavered in her emotion. "It was an enormous shift, huge; for the first time ever, my sister saw that she was really okay. The most amazing part is, five days after she'd had her breakthrough, she went to her husband, and said, 'You know, all this diagnosis, and saying that I'm broken, I don't think it's true.'"

Sam continued, "My sister's husband, who was also suffering with a great deal of work-related stress, saw the change in his wife, and agreed with what his wife was seeing. For the first time in his life, he also was in a different space, with more peace of mind.

"I have absolutely no idea what I said," Sam emphasized. "I feel it was the faith I have that neither one of them is broken. You know, Elsie, I'm usually very careful to share only the feeling, because it was a family member, and I know it's not

Elsie Spittle

my job to coach unless that door is really opened. It was a huge learning for me. My sister couldn't even tell me what I said. I told her, 'I don't know what I said either.'"

Elsie: "Oh, my goodness. That's a beautiful story, Sam. I love the fact that none of you really know what was said, and yet the change that occurred for your sister and husband is undeniable. And if that doesn't speak to Syd saying throughout his teaching years, *'You don't have to understand this to benefit.'*

"Sam, your story is such a clear example of this. You don't know what you said, your sister and her husband don't know what you said, yet the results speak for themselves. Your whole family must have been so touched by the change in your sister and her husband."

Sam nodded, with tears in her eyes, too emotional to speak. We sat in silence for a time together on screen, savoring the moment, then ended the call.

Two weeks later, I had a follow up call with Sam. She was bubbling over with good feelings. "Elsie, I can't get over our last call. When I shared the story of my sister and her husband's transformation, telling you the story made it more visible in my life. And when you mentioned Syd's teaching about it being unnecessary to understand the Principles and yet we'll benefit anyway, well, I had kind of forgotten that.

Mentored by Mind

"I realized more deeply that when we share, it's not about the words; it's about the feeling. As I mentioned before, I have been doing this work with myself, and helping others for many years now. And although I often still feel I don't have the words to articulate my understanding, I now feel okay with that. I found my voice inside me, and know when to listen, and when to share. I'm so grateful for our coaching sessions, Elsie, because most of all, I have found more trust in myself, and I know what the right direction is."

Elsie: "Sam, all of us can feel the emotion more than the words. I feel what is coming through you; that feeling is expressing your learning. That's what I felt so deeply when Victoria said, 'the page before the words.' I got such a deep sense of the truth."

Sam: "Yes, for a long time, I kind of felt that I was alone with this learning, and then I listened to you, and found the feeling within myself. Then I realized that I was never alone; that I am always connected to my true nature, from within."

Elsie: "That's a very deep insight. Honestly, Sam, I'm not saying this lightly; if what you just shared now is the only thing you learned, that insight would guide you through the rest of your life. That is how profound that insight is."

Spiritual Energy is Everything

After my call with Sam, I found myself continuing to reflect on our conversation. I was very moved by what Sam shared, about how she was trusting and listening to her own wisdom more of the time.

This is such a key issue with many of those I mentor. They often listen to others more than themselves, and will ask me pointed questions about how to articulate their understanding, how to build their coaching business, whether they are ready to coach others, and so on. They often have a difficult time believing they have the answers and guidance within their own psyche.

Once I've listened deeply and gotten a sense of my client's reality, I find myself asking them, "What about listening to yourself?"

Their response usually is, "Listening to myself? Oh yes, yes, I do listen to myself, but I'm not really sure whether I'm listening to my wisdom or my ego intellect."

I know that the phrase "listen to yourself" can be hard for us to hear, because when we think of listening to ourselves, that may sound ego driven. However, I want you to really hear this: I'm not talking about listening to the personal self. I'm talking about listening to our Divine self. Honor that privilege.

Mentored by Mind

It was what I was pointing to at the beginning chapter of Part Three when I wrote about Ian and Evelyn, the couple who shared their health recovery story, and how people were being so drawn into their experience that they were forgetting their own experience, their own journey, their own being.

When we forget to honor our Divinity, our spiritual birthright, we are forgetting the most important fact of all. Everything is spiritual energy, and spiritual energy is everything. When we honor that spiritual gift, the light shines brightly, not only in us, but in those we come in contact with who may have forgotten who they are "inside."

I have a perfect example to share about a business leader and coach I'd been talking with. Lars is a strong leader, successful in his coaching business, and was open to sharing his vulnerability with refreshing candor.

In our call, Lars related an experience he'd had with a client a few weeks ago, in the context of a leadership program not explicitly based on the Three Principles. "She was from Ireland," Lars told me, "and had very strong religious beliefs. I don't quite know what we talked about or what led her to confide that she'd come to the program feeling that she was broken."

Lars paused as he gathered his thoughts. "Toward the end of the training, she told us, 'Now I know I'm okay; I'm

Elsie Spittle

reconnected with source.' It was so beautiful and powerful, and we all had a warm deep connection. But then something happened within me, when I saw that she literally lit up in front of me and the whole room, and everyone was like, 'Wow, the light came on.'"

Once again, Lars hesitated before he continued. "I don't really know how to say this, other than I remember in that moment, something closed in me. I think I got scared; maybe the power of this essence? It was like this woman utterly transformed in front me and the group. We all felt it, and then I was like whoa, and something inside of me got tight. It's a few weeks now, but I can still get that same sensation in my body. Elsie, I'm curious what comes up for you as I tell you this. Does this make any sense to you? Do you resonate with this at all?"

Elsie: "Lars, first of all, let me say that I really respect your honesty. Thank you for sharing that story with me.

"I have experienced that sense of tightness and of fear. I experienced that for a year and a half with Syd, when he first shared his Enlightenment experience with Ken and me. I'm not sure how to say this, so bear with me, Lars, while I try to express the inexpressible.

"That light you saw emanating from your client is her core essence. We all have that essence within us. Another way of

Mentored by Mind

saying that is, the essence is spiritual energy, and spiritual energy is everything, both form and formless. We're all part of that infinite spiritual energy.

"And every now and then, when we experience the grandness, the enormity, the profundity of this energy of everything, damn right it can scare us! Our human nature bows before the magnitude of the inexpressible.

"It's natural, from time to time, for our human nature to be in awe of this powerful energy. When I was experiencing that with Syd, sometimes his presence would be too much for me. Certainly, his presence was far too much for me when I hid from him that fateful day, when I ultimately uncovered my first insight.

"There were times, even after I'd had my first insight and begun my journey, when I'd be in a low mood, and Syd might pop by for a cup of tea or a chat. And it would almost be painful, Lars, being with him when I was in such a low mood. I was judging myself for my state of mind, and in my lostness, I was thinking that Syd was also judging me.

"He wasn't feeling like that at all. He was viewing me with unconditional love. He saw my fear and went beyond it; he was centered in his being. But his unconditional love was too strong for me. Given his level of understanding, and his kindness, when he saw how I was struggling, he'd have a quick cuppa, give me a hug, then off he'd go.

"Later on, that afternoon or the next morning, his wife, Barb, would come by to see how I was doing. She didn't have quite the same power. It wasn't as strong; it was a bit softer, and I could be with her in my low mood. I could sort of look at her out of the corner of my eye; it was like I was still in hiding.

"Whereas with Syd, when I was feeling low, I couldn't look at him directly; the power was too strong. I'd duck my head; I couldn't really be with him.

"So, Lars, in response to your question of whether I resonate with your story, I do understand that tight feeling of fear. And I'm going to circle back to the power of Consciousness—noticing. The fact that you noticed that, Lars, is what's most important.

"And the second most important thing is your vulnerability. I have such respect for that quality in you. Here you are, a big macho male, and you have the courage to just share what you've noticed. What you see. That's tremendous."

Lars spoke up, "But I still felt the fear, Elsie! Why would I feel fear when someone lights up from within?"

Mentored by Mind

I could see that Lars was still feeling anxious and judgmental about himself. "Stop trying to figure it out, Lars. I honor what you're noticing, and I minimize your fear. Just disregard it, Lars. Yep, just disregard it. Honor what happened in your conversation with your client, the woman who was then moved to share the words, 'I'm reconnected with source' with the whole room and the room lit up. Wow. Go there. Go to that space, and more of that will happen, and you'll get used to that powerful energy. After all, it was through the conversation between you both that she was led to wake up to who she is 'inside.'

"That's our journey. Getting used to who we really are. Isn't that a funny thing to say? Imagine that we have to get used to the purity of who we are on the inside. But it's true. It's true.

"We're all beautiful souls. And we don't give ourselves very much credit for being such wise souls, Lars. I want you to rest in that feeling more. It's powerful to know we're all connected on a spiritual level. That becomes visible when something profound happens, as you describe what took place with your client in the leadership class.

"The exchange that happened between you all, as a group, is a profound, inspiring example. It speaks to the richness of our own being. I don't know how else to say it, Lars,

Elsie Spittle

and I trust that the feeling behind my words will convey what I mean.

"Bottom line, we're our own best friend. No matter how much we love our spouse or partner, or family or whomever; bottom line, we come into this world alone, and we leave this world alone. No matter who is surrounding us, or what souls are surrounding us.

"That's why it's so important to get to know the inner 'me.' When we know who we are on the inside, we're never alone. Wherever we go in the world, we're safe. When you were witnessing and acknowledging the power of that spiritual energy, Lars, you said it took you aback. Now you're realizing that's the power of who we are, at a core level. That's the power we can count on. That's what we honor."

Lar's was sitting motionless, and his face was peaceful, quite different from the stress that had been visible earlier. "Lars, do you want to add anything?

Lars: "I was having a really bad day; talking with you has been really nice and helped my thinking settle. I just want to say thanks to you, Elsie, because you've made a big difference for me in the moment."

Elsie: "And who else are you going to thank?"

Lars looked puzzled, "My client?"

Mentored by Mind

Elsie: "And?"

Lars: "Myself, I guess"

Elsie: "All right!! Yay!! Yes, yourself. Because you had a choice, Lars. You had a choice where you could have stayed in that tough day feeling, and you didn't. You went to a better space."

Lars: "It might not be gone completely, but I can sit in it a little more comfortably."

Elsie: "Yep, there you go. Bless your heart, Lars. Thank you again for sharing your humility and the beauty of seeing the light within us all. When we see that light, it's like being uplifted by our true nature. When we're resting in our true nature, we're resting in integrity, and we don't need confirmation about whether we're right or wrong. We know.

"Lars, one last thing I want to add before our call is finished. In our short conversation today, we were able to share and learn in shorthand. We lived in the moment, and we both gained insight.

"That's a beautiful thing, not only for us as individual souls, but what we then share with the world. Just by being, sharing love and compassion. 'The page before the words.' Thank you, Lars, it's been an absolute pleasure to have time with you."

Epilogue

My last chapter is entitled, *Spiritual Energy is Everything*, and I am moved to end my stories by deepening that topic. We ARE what we are looking for. We have everything we need to thrive in life, to have peace of mind and contentment, to rise to the occasional life challenges we all come across. We are Love. We are *Mentored by Mind*.

To realize that we are mentored by Mind is such an incredible gift that I simply don't have words to express what an honor and privilege it is to realize that spiritual fact. I will say once again, to know that we ARE what we're looking for. To never have to search for answers again, knowing that all the answers are within us already. An open mind, heart, and soul are all that is needed to rest in Love, to have soul-to-soul conversations, where we are students together, united in harmony.

This is how we contribute to humanity, sharing our understanding of the Three Principles, and where they originated from. Sydney Banks uncovered the mystery of life during his enlightenment in 1973. Syd shared the spiritual gifts he uncovered without hesitation, with absolute certainty that what he'd seen in a timeless moment of Oneness would help alleviate humanity's suffering. Never once did he question his spiritual journey, never once did he hesitate to help those in need, never once did he say, "*Follow me.*"

Syd always pointed us within, to our own innate wisdom, to our own spiritual nature. He encouraged us to *"listen to the feeling"* of our true nature. He encouraged us to *"just live."* What could be simpler than that?

Further Reading

Genesis of the Three Principles: Reflections on the Life and Discoveries of Sydney Banks is now available.

https://www.amazon.com/dp/1702631303

Syd's website archived. www.sydneybanks.org

Link for Books, Audios and Videos by Sydney Banks:

http://sydbanks.com/

More digital and books of Sydney Banks can be found here:

https://books.apple.com/us/author/sydney-banks/id1141097963

Resources

3 Principles for Human Development (Elsie's website)

www.3phd.net

Three Principles Foundation (hosts the School on Salt Spring Island)

www.threeprinciplesfoundation.org

Your own wisdom!

Acknowledgements

My heartfelt gratitude to Lynn Spittle and Kim Patriquin. Lynn designed the cover, with Kim's help, and formatted this book. I don't have the words to express how much it means to have them both working with me. Not only are they a tremendous help, but they inspire me with their creativity and their love of learning new things. They've opened the mind of this senior to more love of learning new things as well, including technology, which has long been my nemesis. . . and now, not so much anymore.

And always, so much gratitude for Ken, my husband of 58 years, for his steadfast support and patient listening to my ideas for the next chapter, or to hear my latest insight, which often prompts an even deeper interpretation from him. Still waters run deep in this lovely man.

And of course, Jane Tucker, for her dedication to editing my material in a way that retains the originality of my words, and adds a final polish to the completed book.

Lastly, deep appreciation for you, the readers, for your continued interest and support. Thank you!

Manufactured by Amazon.ca
Acheson, AB

13354287R00072